Forged in Fire

Applying Godly Principles to Daily Life

Forged in Fire

Applying Godly Principles to Daily Life

By

Dr. Freddy B. Wilson

The opinions expressed by the author are not necessarily those of Wilsonet Enterprises

Published by Wilsonet Enterprises

135 Bonnie Lane | Fayetteville, Georgia 30215 USA

404-754-0858 |

Wilsonet Enterprises is committed to excellence.

Cover design by Dr. Freddy B. Wilson

Cover photo by Public Domain

Bio photo by Dr. Freddy B. Wilson

Published in the United States of America

ISBN: 978-0-9987873-6-7

1. Religion / Christian Life / Personal Growth / Faith

2. Family And Relationship/General

17.4.20

Forged in Fire – Applying Godly Principles to Daily Life

Most of us have heard the expression that iron sharpens iron. That usually applies to have an iron-hard person sharpen you as an iron-hard Christian. If you didn't know, sharp objects like swords and knives are heated up to create its hardened and sharp surface. In other words, they are forged in fire! I believe it's not just people that help sharpen us as Christians, but also the daily experiences we face in life. This is especially so when we learn from our experiences. Our takes from our experiences should be ones that helped grow us as human beings and not create prejudices, preconceived notions, and biases. Through my experiences and education, I discovered one of my purposes is the write. I wish it had not taken so long to get to this realization. I thought about getting into the recording industry (Gospel and Religious) but I wondered if it was too late in life to do so. I do know that when God tells you to do something, you must obey. You will be truly blessed though! This does not mean you won't have to go through something to get where God wants you to go.

This book is about various experiences in my life that sharpened me as a Christian and helped build my faith. I was forged in fire to become the person I am today. This occurred as I applied Godly principles to all the things I had to face. Having a personal relationship with God was instrumental in my ability to hear His voice and abide by His instructions and also doing things I wanted to do while staying in His will. The stories I'm about to discuss are but several of the things I've dealt with while living for Christ.

The Journey Begins

In 25 January 2009, I attended some military training at Fairchild Air Force Base (AFB), WA, preparing for my deployment to Iraq. At 49 and still doing military deployments as a civilian I wondered if I was still in the right job. I enjoyed doing my job but wondered if it was time to move on. I had to reflect on my life and realized sometimes we have to look at ourselves and see what we're doing with our lives and what we've become. Questions to ask are:

1. Are we happy with ourselves and what we're doing?
2. Could we do better at what we're doing?
3. Are we willing to make a change?
4. What would you be doing if we had options?
5. What are we willing to sacrifice to make needed changes?
6. How do we value our experiences?

Here's something to ponder: What are you doing today in your yesterday space? This doesn't only apply to your job or your career. You have to take account of your personal relationship with others and your relationship with God.

That same year I came up with a motto for myself: "Heavenly Inspired, God Blessed". This applies to all facets of my life. I do agree that what you think of yourself is what you become. Be very careful about your approach to problems and the things you think. Men and women must be accountable and maintain accountability for their thoughts.

Men, sometimes the things in our hearts will manifest in our minds. We must keep lust in check or it will take over our willpower. If we don't dismiss the thought with God's help, then we will find ourselves attempting to go after our physical desires for women outside our marriage or actually committing adultery. If it's too late to not commit adultery, it's never too late to turn to God for forgiveness and getting back on the right track. If your wife is aware of your sin, you must ask her for forgiveness and assure her you will work to regain her trust. You must first forgive yourself after God forgives you.

Moving When God Says to Move

I've traveled all over the world and most of the United States. I get to meet people, young and old, single and married. When I meet single people many of them speak of the frustration of meeting someone nice to whom they would one day marry. Some of them have become impatient and want things to move along quickly. This sometimes can lead to people settling for less in a mate that what God will have for them. I usually encourage these people to wait on God for a mate.

You should start out as friends. You can practice your social skills by talking to old friends. I talked to an old female friend of mine back in 2014. We talked a bit and it was good catching up. There was no intent on hooking up or anything intimate. We were able to talk with no strings attached and nothing sexual in nature was ever discussed. God showed me how lust could have ruined my life. Having a new friend will be good as long as I keep things in perspective.

Throughout trials and tribulations your faith should remain in God. Even when there are disappointments such as being late for a plane trip or problems with your rental car or hotel reservations. It all has purpose. During one of my trips, I faced disappointment. The airline on which I traveled lost my weapon at the airport. I had to travel on to my hotel without the weapon in hopes they would find it later. On my way to my hotel in Fayetteville, NC, the hotel called to say my room had been cancelled due to a family displaced by fire. I really wanted to stay at that hotel, which is nicer than the replacement hotel; however, I did have some sympathy for the family that could not return to their home. Disappointment is never pleasant but many times serves its purposes.

Sometimes I must realize that when things happen it's not always just about me. It could be a plan to bless others at that time or at a later date. I must place myself and my problem in God's hands and trust Him. At any given time, I must realize that God has a blessing in store for my family. Whatever it is it's beyond the extra money that can be made from your job! God is so good even if you don't look at the material things. Just still being alive after all we've been through is proof enough of how good God is.

If you know me, you would know how important family is to me. During my travels in 2009 I visited one of my sisters at her son's house outside of Fayetteville, NC. It was good getting to see my sister, her son, and his family. I'm proud of what this nephew has accomplished in his life despite disappointments including a failed first marriage. My nephew and I talked and we agreed that you have to trust God during the trials of life. When God tells you to do something you have to do it; no matter how foolish it may seem to others. I think God has blessed my nephew with insight and that's what keeps him going forward. I wished one of my other nephews would give his life to God and see the benefits.

Flash forward to 2015 and my nephew called me about some job opportunity he had but was perplexed for it would mean he had to move away from his family to Jacksonville, FL. We prayed about it and I told him that God will bless him during his time away from the family as along as he remained in God's will. I later found out that as a result of his work at this job, he received a promotion to another location in Tennessee. By the time he and his wife decided they should come together at his new location (2016) after he'd been there for over seven months, he was offered another position in Fayetteville, NC. Therefore, he didn't have to move his family and could remain in the family home of which they were purchasing. It's amazing how he could not find a good position before he left Fayetteville, NC but did as God would have him do and he came back in a supervisory position. God will provide for you when you're willing to do what He tells you to do and step out of your comfort zone.

Now, back to 2009. During some training in early 2009, I discovered it was better than what I thought it would be! Sometimes the things we perceive to be a problem could turn out to be blessings. We must stay tuned to the plan God has for our lives. Once he puts you in the fight, He will fight your battles. The devil is waging war on our minds.

I had many thoughts during my travels in 2009. I even began to question my love life. Sometimes I ask myself what is real love? I thought Chris Rock's movie, "I Think I Love My Wife", was a stupid title. Now I don't know if it's so stupid. I can truly say I love my wife. I do ask if I got to know her like I know her now, would I have married her? I bought India Arie's new album and it made me realize why I have all her albums. I love her spirit and I can see and hear the God in her. I'm not fantasizing about India Arie but realized you don't have to know someone personally to love their spirit. I realized I need to show the love for my wife's spirit.

On 13 February 2009, I realized how much I really loved my wife. Sometimes when couples go through their ups and downs it's easy to forget what brought you together and sometimes what's keeping them together. The previous night I woke up in the middle of the night. I was thinking of sex and had to realize that since my wife not being here, it's out of the question. Men should not lust for women who are not their wives. I pray God gives me strength to remain strong.

On 14 February 2009 (Valentine's Day), I spent most of today by myself. My wife seemed to be having a hard time being by herself. I would have preferred to have been with her. God is continually assuring me that everything will be alright. I just want my life to be in the will of God. I pray God will use me to spread His Word in my special way, however that may be.

On 15 February 2009, I thanked God for my being able to worship in a spirit-filled church while I was away from home. I heard a song from India Arie that says the worst disease in the world is hate. The cure for hate is love. I think this is quite true. I watched the movie, "Fire Proof" at my nephew and his wife's house. This movie presents a lot of truths in a Christian's daily walk. It covers a myriad of topics such as gossip, infidelity, temptation, and the need for devotion to marriage. The only danger I see is some folks watching this movie is that some might want to apply these principles to long-term live-in situations, instead of marriage. If you're living with someone long-term and not married, and see problems in the person, marrying them will only amplify the problem and push you deeper in regret.

Some folks, particularly women, will accept or overlook problems in or with a person just to keep from being alone. You can be married and still feel alone. From personal experience, there's not much worse than having a mate and still feel lonely. I had a wonderful sharing the Lord with my nephew and his family.

On 16 February 2009, I awoke refreshed as to how good God is. I am expecting miracles to happen this week and in the next few months as well as the next year. God has blessed with a friend that we can talk about everything. God has also blessed me with a wife who loves me and will try to do anything to please. She is one of reasons I don't have to look outside my marriage for satisfaction. Our only major problem was a weak friendship that is now growing.

God has blessed my family in so many ways. Our struggles were easing off. I prayed that God gave my family peace during my absence while deployed. I continually asked the Lord what's in His will for me to do. I prayed that God helped me in my weaknesses. I hadn't done much writing on my other two books then. I worked on getting my friend Joyce to sign the contract on our joint book deal. I knew my first book would do well for the Lord has purposed it. My nephew Ken and his wife Martha agreed to distribute my book in their bookstore at their church.

While I was deployed to Afghanistan in 2009, I often found out what a struggle it was to keep from succumbing to weaknesses. I only wanted to stay in God's will so I prayed he gave me strength. Keep in mind that God is aware of each step we take. I prayed that God will take my weaknesses away. Being outside the Will of God is just a waste of time. It takes away from doing Godly things. The pleasure we get from worldly things is only temporary. The things we do for God will last an eternity. Don't waste time on shallow things or habits. I often pray, "Lord, teach me what you want me to know, show me what you want me to be, mold me. Please give me the strength to walk in the way you want me to walk. Give me a clean heart and take away anything that is not like you."

Staying Obedient

At different times in my life I felt God had something special for me to do. I prayed, "Lord, please show me clearly what you want me to do!" In 2009, my job posted new assignments and I wondered if I should apply for the leadership position at my position in Atlanta. That location had gone through a lot of changes at that time and I didn't think I was in the best political position to get such a job. I wondered if all this preparation me was going through was to bless me. I didn't get the position and they brought in someone else to be the supervisor. It wasn't until much later I realized that God was molding me to become more confident in my work and experience.

We have to get over our pride and self-motivators. There's nothing wrong in wanting a certain thing or a certain position on a job. We have to pray and then trust God to place us in the right positions at the right times. Beware of low self-esteem hidden in self-pity! This is especially true if you're single or divorced and looking for a mate. You may be faithful and look to God for help finding a mate but you still have to be careful not to take things into your own hands. For example, if you meet someone you'd like to get to know well, that person may not respond to you in kind.

We have a tendency to go after that person and disregard warning signs. If a relationship doesn't get started, we wonder what is wrong with us. We will think that others don't want us as we are and begin to lower our standards and our just tolerances. When we meet someone else, we might allow them to treat us in ways we would have never allowed before. Don't allow sub-standard or ungodly people in your lives just to keep from being lonely. First start loving yourself and let God work on you before getting in a relationship with someone else. Everything you need is in God's house.

I found out in February 2009 that God had blessed my long-term friend with a new car. I thank God for blessing my friend with a new car with zero percent interest and lower payments. Never be envious when God is blessing someone else. You should be happy for them and not compare them to your circumstances. I know God can bless you when you least expect and in ways unimaginable! I love God with all of my might and so should you!

Comparing yourself to others can create self-doubt and sometimes depression. Sometimes when you're down you have to look to God for strength. The devil wants us to be down on ourselves so he can creep in and stop you from seeking God. If the devil can distract you, he can divert you from the path that God intended. I watched Tyler Perry tonight on Larry King Live. I was inspired that he only went for doing what he loved and not the money! Too many people are seeking the mighty dollar in all they do. I pray that God keeps me grounded and on the right path. God is my "all in all" and I need him to keep me grounded. I ask the Lord to help me avoid distractions. I know TV is a big distraction while I'm away from home. I don't get to watch much TV while I'm home but I know it can slow me down there as well. On Larry King, Dolly Parton just said, "Sometimes you have to toot your own horn. If not, some folks won't know you're coming!" I'm not comfortable tooting my own horn. I feel if I do as the Lord will have me do, any recognition I need will come.

Here comes the point I'm always preaching about – obedience. I researched obedience and I realized again that I'm where I am today by remaining obedient to the Lord. I pray that God continues to show me His Will and that I strive to stay in God's Will.

Speaking of being obedient, I'm sure you've heard my story of how God blessed us with our house in Fayetteville, GA. When I told the story, I mentioned how in 2006 God blessed us with a higher interest mortgage on the house in Fayetteville while the house in Williamsburg, VA still hadn't sold. After a good study on 1 Corinthians, I learned that my body is a temple unto the Lord. It's time I treat it as such – completely! When you get yourself in order this way, God will bless you, especially when you remain in His will. In regards to how God blessed us when we moved into our house in Fayetteville, GA, here's the rest of the story. We were praying for God to bless us to sell our home in Williamsburg, VA so we could close on our house in Fayetteville. When that wasn't working, the family changed its prayers to, Lord just make a way – He did! We were able to close on our new house with a higher interest, ARM, with a first and second mortgage. I told my wife that if this was God blessing us, then we would never have to make a payment on this new high-interest loan. Through many trials and tribulations, God blessed us to sell the old house, then close on the new, lower fixed-rate loan on the new house one day before the payment was due on the high-interest loan. God is so good!

God can and will bless you over anything that wants to stop you. Truly, if you place your care in God's hands, He can bless you to get over whatever your enemy puts in your way. After I got my family situated in the new house in Fayetteville, GA, I had to deploy to Afghanistan to a position lower than my paygrade. My stateside boss asked me what I was doing for a job there. When I emailed him back that I'd been placed in a supervisory position, he never responded! God knows I didn't fully know what his problem was but I hoped he got over it.

While I was in Afghanistan, I thanked God that my family seemed to be doing well. I prayed that they too prayed to God nightly and knew that He is a comfort. When I face a challenge, from here out I will pray that God equips me to face the challenge and He guides me through it. No more will I face any challenge on my own.

My experiences in my job in Virginia and while I was deployed taught me that my security is in God and not in my government job. It was the Lord that blessed me with this job and it is the Lord that keeps me steadfast! I feel I was sent to Afghanistan in a "worker bee" capacity but the people there put me in a supervisory role. God is so good! It's not that working in a worker bee capacity is bad, it's just demeaning with a person with a much job experience that I had at the time.

My wife complained to me about some people on her job. I told her to take her eyes off the problems on her job and to place her cares in God's hands. This spiritual warfare is the fight Christians should be prepared to fight. Once you discover your Godly purposes, don't let anyone stop you from doing it. My writing about my experiences only confirms my purpose is to write for the Lord. I want to keep writing for the Lord. I want the whole world to know how good God is.

Other parts of your life will be affected by your walk with God. While I was away in Afghanistan, my son's birthday approached. He emailed me to let me know he understood how I sacrificed to take care of the family. It's amazing how he's becoming a fine young man. I owe it all to God for taking care of me and my family.

I thank God for allowing me to have a wife that can take care of things while I'm away from home. On my way to my deployment to Afghanistan, God blessed to remain in North Carolina to take care of matters with our money before I left the country. My wife told me the IRS had wrote us a note stating why we got more money than we expected. Regardless, this is the kind of blessing only God can do. It's called favor. He has shown His favor once again! I think this is for my being obedient and faithful. God has dominion over all the earth and can give us anything He wants us to have. You do have to watch the way you're living or it'll all come back to you. I often pray, "God, please show me what to do next and every day."

I know it's hard to understand as we experience difficulties but I will have you know God is aware of all we go through and it all has purpose. During my travels on my deployment, I was stranded in a different location for eight days. I didn't understand the purpose but God was working miracles! Before I left on the trip, I was sharing a very small space with a roommate. He had the larger side of the room. My side was so small I had no room to set up my laptop so I could type. I came back and found out my roommate was gone! I'm not none-sociable but I didn't have much space on my side of the room. His side afforded storage beneath the bed. Thank God for then I was able to start back on my writing on the computer. It was time to start exercising, too.

I often witness to others, including my neighbors as to how good God is. I am able to say this for I felt in the midst of my financial trouble I believed God would prevail! God later blessed my wife to move me to take a step with some smaller insurance policies. The money from these helped me work some financial issues before I deployed. As the extra money from the deployment began to come in, I tithed off the top and let God show me what to do with the rest. My neighbor was going through some things as her husband was laid off from his job. I told the neighbor to put her trust in the Lord and not be distracted by the problems in the economy. I told her if she stayed in God's will, He will deliver them from any problems. I later found out from my neighbor her husband got a better job and has been working ever since. Trust only in God and never in what you see! It took me to stop worrying about me credit report and let God bless me financially. God is my all!

I overheard a conversation when I walked into my office the other day. One person seemed to wonder why folks seek God. Another talked of pagan practices of his heritage with keeping skulls of ancestors on posts to guide them. Another was really confused by speaking of Greek gods. I so wanted to jump in and correct them but I learned some time ago Christians should not jump into large group discussions where you could be made to look a fool. I asked the Lord to give me an opportunity to speak His word on an individual basis. I asked He gives me the right word to say at the right time. People are really hurting to know the Lord. I know each of these people are living their own hell right now in their personal circumstances. I prayed for God to help them no matter their religious beliefs, or lack thereof.

While I was deployed, I was able to attend a fine gospel service on base. I was surprised and glad to see the number of folks there to serve the Lord! I always liked being able to worship the Lord no matter where I am. I will continue to seek the Lord. I found myself sentimental about a Bible my mother gave to me many years ago. Somehow, I lost it when I traveled through North Carolina before I deployed. Though it seemed hopeless, I called back and asked the staff there to look for my Bible. I found out later that they found my Bible and said they would have someone bring it to me. I thank God for this because I felt bad about losing my Bible. I specifically like the case it is in. It took a little while before they got my Bible back to me. I still have that Bible today.

Having Faith While Working Through Distractions

The devil will place distractions in your life to keep you from doing what God will have you do. I found that if you take a small detour from where you ought to be, it could lead to a long road of distractions from the Lord. The Lord let me see what other folks were up to that might be working against me. Even though I was initially angry about these people I chose to pray for these folks and not plot to work against them. I began exercise to include running and lost 2 lbs. I pray that God keeps me healthy and that I would have a healthy weight loss and continue to steadily do it. I found another prayer that helped – "Lord, fill me with your Word and your Way."

While I was deployed, my wife asked me to jointly write with her a book about family. I thought it was good idea and I told her how to get started. I pray God leads us to do and say the right things.

One thing I realized in 2009 is that Christians were under attack! It seemed OK then and now that people respect other religions but as soon as you speak about Christ, people want to label you as crazy or a religious fanatic. As soon as some folks that honor Buddha or other idols find or think that you're a Christian, they will try to go after you personally or professionally. Don't be alarmed! This is an attack of the devil but he can't win. Just call on the name of the Lord and He will protect you and fight your battles. Overcome the urge to immediately respond to these attacks. Ask the Lord what to do and what to say, if needed. Oftentimes you don't even have to say anything to the offender. Sometimes it's best to let them think they have won. Count on the Lord and He will lead you to victory. Deuteronomy 32:35 (NLT) says, "I will take revenge; I will pay them back. In due time their feet will slip. Their day of disaster will arrive, and their destiny will overtake them."

In 2009 I was still working on writing my second book. I prayed that God showed me when to pay for the new book to be published. I knew I needed to do it while I was away. God put my family on higher ground sooner than I expected. I prayed the Lord to bless to say the right things to inspire folks every day.

I was initially hesitant to tell others to have faith in God for I didn't want them to think I was crazy. I learned that you should never be ashamed of your relationship and faith in

22

God. You don't have to push your faith on others but you should not be afraid to say where you stand. A young man and I talked a lot during our deployment to Iraq. I mentioned to him many times about the good things that have happened to us was only due to God's blessings and not luck. We started out one night to get a Space Available (Space-A) flight out of our assigned station but we got bumped! This means we were not going on the flight we expected. As the guy who would transport us back to our camp was taking us back, he made a stop at the aircraft for which we were refused. I told the young man traveling with me that the guy might be trying to get us on the flight anyway. The guy did not tell us what he was doing. As it turned out, I was right! But unfortunately, no matter how hard he tried, the guy could not get us on either of the flights going straight to Germany. He later told us there was a flight later in the morning but it goes to Qatar. We had already been informed that the unit in Qatar responsible for assisting us getting flights out of Qatar to Germany was temporarily not providing assistance for the next week. The guy helping us, a senior US Army non-commissioned officer, said he would do what he could for us. God worked through this guy to get the unit in Qatar to agree to only transport us from a base in Qatar to Doha International Airport. We ended up meeting a young Air Force airman, who we found out was going home on emergency leave due to the death of his father. I was able to talk to this young man and calm his nerves before he

23

flew out to the US. I think it was meant to be for me to talk to this troubled young man to whom I assured God would give him peace. The guy in Qatar did more for us than promised by fast-tracking us there through customs, providing us a nice room so we could shower and change, and then transported us to the airport. We were blessed to get a flight out of Qatar early the next day.

God blessed us with a nice flight from Qatar to Germany. We then got a taxi from the city to the air base. Unfortunately, the taxi cost $300! We knew of no other way to get there. The guy I was traveling with paid. That taxi only took us to the gate. I paid for the taxi from the gate to billeting office. We were told all the rooms at the new facility were booked but the airman that helped us got us rooms by the Officer's Club. We were blessed with suites! These room were really nice. I was later asked by one of our area managers who was supposed to be assisting us how we managed to get a flight out of Qatar that fast. He thought we would not get out as soon as we did. That's how good God is and you can't always explain how God works. I think the guy I was traveling with then saw how God blesses those that believe. In this case, me. I gave God all the glory. We also managed to book a couple of rooms in a nice hotel where the guy I was traveling with stayed in Fayetteville, NC before we went to Iraq. God continued to bless us. I could hardly wait to see my family again.

While in Germany our adviser told us that there was no counselor available, which was required before we could leave; however, God made a way and the adviser made us an appointment for the next day. The session went well and our adviser took us to get our plane tickets. When we got our tickets, we were not provided seat assignments for flights from Germany to Atlanta.

We got to meet some of our senior leadership while we were there and I got to talk to some old associates of mine who had been blessed to be in command positions. I think this is more than coincidence and we were blessed to greet our command's future commander. We got a short tour of Germany. We had lunch at an authentic German restaurant. The food was good and this restaurant was nice. We walked around and I took lots of pictures. This all was amazing! God amazes me sometimes!

We finally got to depart the base to head home. We had to catch the shuttle to the airport at 4:45am. When we got to the airport, the person I was travelling with was blessed to be able to go to a business class seat and he did not have to wait. I had to wait in line. My blessing was that the airline agent checked and was able to get me a window seat on an exit row. That gave me plenty of room to move around on our 10-hour flight. The guy traveling with me did not have a seat assignment until we got to the gate. He was blessed to get an aisle seat.

The Need for Wisdom

Psalm 113 tells us to praise the Lord for He provides. Unfortunately, many of us think we have to understand everything that goes on in our lives. If you have wisdom, you'd know that we won't understand everything that occurs, especially when God is working in our lives. Proverbs 3:5-6 tells us to not depend on our own understanding. Proverbs 3:13-18 tells us about the benefits of wisdom.

Godly wisdom will take us further in life than any other kind of wisdom. Other wisdom may be able to get you to some places but it won't be able to keep you there. Isaiah 56:1-2 (NIV) talks about salvation for Others. [1] This is what the LORD says: "Maintain justice and do what is right, for my salvation is close at hand and my righteousness will soon be revealed. [2] Blessed is the one who does this—the person who holds it fast, who keeps the Sabbath without desecrating it, and keeps their hands from doing any evil."

Isaiah 56:10-12 (NIV) discusses a lack of knowledge: [10] Israel's watchmen are blind, they all lack knowledge; they are all mute dogs, they cannot bark; they lie around and dream, they love to sleep. [11] They are dogs with mighty appetites; they never have enough. They are shepherds who lack understanding; they all turn to their own way; they seek their own gain.

It's better to have wisdom than to act with folly. Ecclesiastes 10:1 shows how we can go from wisdom to folly. Ecclesiastes 10:1 (NLT) says, "As dead flies cause even a bottle of perfume to stink, so a little foolishness spoils great wisdom and honor. Ecclesiastes 10:2 (NLT) says a wise person chooses the right road; a fool takes the wrong one. We really have to get our acts together so we can understand and use wisdom. Ecclesiastes 9:18 (NLT) says, "Better to have wisdom than weapons of war, but one sinner can destroy much that is good. Be careful about how you interact with others and the way you handle your personal and professional business.

Sometimes it's hard to stay in the Will of God. I know God has blessed me to be able to write and he wants me to write about his glory. Back on 10 November 2009, I noted I had been trying to get back to writing in my book for many months. Lord knows I had a lot on my mind at that time. I really loved the time I spent writing when I was deployed. When I got home, there were too many demands on my time. At that time, I was at work for 9 to 10 hours. I spent at least 2 hours a day commuting, and I had to check homework with the girls before and sometimes after dinner. By the time I sat down at my computer, I was really tired. So, I only did a little bit of writing at a time.

When I finished writing my first book, the publishing process with Tate Publishing went very slowly. I asked God for the right publisher and I felt I had the right one. So, I knew I must continue to trust God.

Just as I was getting things situated at home and we were getting ready to send our son off to college, I got an odd call from my organization's civilian personnel assignments section. The assignments' representative said I was "quiet" and was checking to see if I was still employed. He said my name was on the vulnerable to move list (VML) for summer 2010. He said my name went on and will come off. I just prayed, "Lord, I need your blessing now!" I didn't want to move again. How many of you know that sometimes your wishes are not what the Lord intends for you? You should pray for what you want but then trust God to give you what's best for you. I didn't have to move during that time or the next few years.

Dealing with Changes in Life

In 2013 there was a change in our organization and they created a position in my Atlanta location that would supervise employees located in different locations in Georgia and Florida. Since neither I nor my current supervisor was chosen for the job and since there were only three authorized positions in my office in Atlanta, one of us three civilian employees had to leave. Since I had been there for nearly seven years, I had been there the longest so that meant I would have to move.

I was frantic! I thought once I finally got a job back home in Atlanta I would never have to leave. I prayed Lord why did this have to happen. I spoke to a friend of mine who was the program manager for my specialty and he told me I had been recommended to lead a unit in Tampa, FL. He thought that was a great opportunity for me and suggested I request and accept the position. Since my wife had a good paying job at that time and our youngest girls were juniors in high school, we decided to leave my family in place and I go to Tampa alone to work the job. With a little faith I decided to allow God to bless me in this new opportunity. Other than being away from my family, this new position ended up being one of the best assignments ever! We should put our trust in God, especially when we're forced to move out of our comfort zones. You never know what God is up to.

In 2015 I was still upset about my credit scores for I felt that creditors had treated me unfairly as I was trying to resolve different accounts. One of them in particular I was paying on but they wouldn't accurately show it in my report. I hired a company to help me in fixing these problems. I was able to slowly but surely pay off the bad debt. I was even able to get one of my credit cards lines increased a little, which bettered my credit score. Through faith in God and asking him how I should approach different financial issues, God blessed me with some of my wants and all of my needs in 2015. Believe it or not most of my financial successes came after I started budgeting to give more money to the church in the way of tithes and offering. I gave nothing out of trying to please people but from what I felt God led me to give.

Then I started having trouble with my usually very reliable car. I told the story of how God blessed me with a 2007 Lexus GS 450h, a hybrid vehicle in 2006. After owning this vehicle for nine years and then living it Florida, it started acting funny when accelerating and giving me strange warning lights. I called my former service adviser in Atlanta about the problems and he told me I needed to get the car to a Lexus dealer as soon as I could. The biggest problem with this at the time was I had no extra money to even pay for a diagnosis. I prayed to God to show me how to take care of this problem. I called the local Lexus dealership in Tampa and scheduled an appointment for Tuesday of the next week. On that previous Friday something told me to take the car to Lexus as a walk-in the next day.

I was just being obedient and didn't fully understand why I was led to take the car in on a Saturday. When I took the car in, I was greeted by someone other than the service representative I was scheduled to see the following week. Sometimes God will put the right person in your path to help you get through some things. The lady informed me that my hybrid battery had gone bad and I had 100,900 miles on the car and one year out of the extended warranty. The lady said she would look through some old history to see if there was a previous complaint while the car was under warranty and she would see what she could do. The only other problem was the guy from Lexus who could make that decision wouldn't be around until the following Tuesday. In the meantime, she put me in a brand-new loaner car.

Lord knows since I didn't buy my car from them and my car was outside the warranty, I wasn't entitled to a loaner car. But God took care of me anyway! This could be nothing but God. But wait, it gets better! After I got home, I did some research of the problem online and found there were many complaints of people who'd had over 100,000 miles on their cars and Lexus refused to fix them under warranty. The average replacement cost was over $6,000. I became concerned for a minute for I knew I didn't have the money to fix it. God told me to be patient and everything would be alright.

I called Lexus on the following Tuesday and got in touch with the Service Adviser I was originally scheduled to see. He confirmed with me that the repair cost was over $6,000 and while the mechanic was looking at my car, he discovered that the accessory battery (the one that works like that in a non-hybrid vehicle) was going bad also. He told me that was the original battery that came in the car. I was amazed that an original battery could last that long. The replacement cost for this battery was over $450. This Service Adviser told me they hadn't talked to the Lexus representative about the problem yet and to give him another day to work the problem.

Long story short, it took nearly the rest of the week to get this problem resolved. I got to drive in a brand-new car for that week. At the end of it all, Lexus agreed to pay for the hybrid battery in full! The Service Adviser gave me a discount on the new accessory battery and God blessed me to pay for it. I was truly amazed at how good God is and how my made a way for me when my money wasn't enough. Favor is so much better than just having money! God can bless you even if you don't have money.

Staying faithful and following God's Will, God blessed me to be able to afford paying my mortgage for our home in Fayetteville, GA and rent in Tampa, FL. God later blessed my wife and me to be approved in 2016 for a loan to purchase a newly constructed luxury townhouse in Tampa with a low affordable deposit. I will discuss this more later. I was concerned about my credit score when we applied for my credit score was low at that time but I found out again that God can bless you regardless of your credit score! God had already blessed me through some upsets as I tried to bring my credit score back up before my wife and I applied for the loan.

Let God Handle Your Problems and Your Issues

Matthew 9:18-22 showed us how Jesus heals in response to faith. During Jesus' time he was being sought to help a father whose daughter had just died. A woman who had suffered for twelve years of bleeding came up behind Jesus and touched his robe. Matthew 9:21 said the woman thought, "If I can just touch his robe, I will be healed." [22]Jesus turned around, and when he saw her, he said, "Daughter, be encouraged! Your faith has made you well." And the woman was healed at that moment!

The woman's faith recognized Jesus' Power. In the same way, Jesus can find and fulfill your every pain. There are three things Christians must remember to do as we go through life.

1. We need to worship God. God continues to bless His people over and over again. God is not only a God of second chances but a God of many chances.

2. Go out and do what the Lord says to do. If you have a close relationship with God you are in

constant communication with Him. When He guides you to do something you need to take heed and do what He asks you to do. Be careful with this for there are other spirits trying to mislead you. You need to learn to know the voice of God.

3. We must learn to wait! However, we want our blessings now! God's timing is not our timing but He'll always bring you out in time. Waiting for our blessings is one of the hardest things we can face as Christians.

You need to know not only who you are but whose you are. God always takes care of His children. Psalms 33:20 says "We put our hope in the LORD." He is our help and our shield. I've learned over the years we should watch and wait.

Waiting on the Lord

I found we have to learn to wait on the Lord as we travel our journeys through life. Isaiah 40:29 says, He gives power to the weak and strength to the powerless. I know personally that sometimes the problems in life can drain you of your strength, both physical and mental. Isaiah 40:31 says, "But those who trust in the LORD will find new strength. They will soar high on wings like eagles. They will run and not grow weary. They will walk and not faint."

We can use the example of eagles to apply to our lives. Eagles stirs up its nest so its young can learn to fly. They spread their wings to warm and protect their young. We need to learn to apply love and understanding to protect our children. Eagles spread their wings to demonstrate to their young how to fly. We need to set an example to our children as to how to live life so they can prepare to enter the world. Even if you are not financially successful, you can at least teach your children good work ethics and how to care for others.

There could be many reasons why we have to wait for God to provide. One reason is that the Glory of God has departed. You are no longer pursuing what God would have for you and you went out on your own. You could have lost the spiritual passion of God. You could also be operating from a defeated position, by disobeying the Word of God.

Some of you are going from church to church, seeing what they can give you. When in actuality you should pray that God place you in the right church where you can make a difference there. You could be living out of flesh, and not out of spirit. Unfortunately, many of us see things for the physical beauty or the status they bring and not for the Glory of God that it could bring.

Some of us try to help God move along by taking on steps without praying or consulting with God first. For example, there might be a certain car that you want but God has not told you to get it and did not allow the financing process of to happen successfully. You then decide to go on your own and do what you want anyway. The problem here is that you jump into a high interest financing deal or the car you buy end up being nothing but trouble. Then you want to blame God for your problems.

Some of us seem to not be able to go through anything, we don't trust God, and we worry. The Bible tells us there will be trouble so why do we freak out when things don't go our way or when something bad happens? We need to trust God for all that is not seen. Some of the things we see are disappointing. We let disappointment blind our sight. Then we reach for things that are not for us. This is especially true in some of our personal relationships.

I suggest you don't be content with the way things are and learn to grow. I've heard somewhere that you'll only succeed greatly if you're willing to fail greatly. When God is telling us to take a chance at something where others have told us we would fail, do it anyway and see how good God is! Some of us let others' opinions affect us. This should never be the case when God is guiding us. The Bible tells us in Ephesians 1:22-23 (NLT), 22 God has put all things under the authority of Christ and has made him head over all things for the benefit of the church. 23 And the church is his body; it is made full and complete by Christ, who fills all things everywhere with himself.

Lamentations 3:24 - 26 (NLT) says, 24 I say to myself, "The LORD is my inheritance; therefore, I will hope in him!

[25] The LORD is good to those who depend on him, to those who search for him. [26] So it is good to wait quietly for salvation from the LORD." Dealing with my children's lives has taught me a lot about waiting. I can give many examples of how God has blessed our children throughout their lives. They may not have seen the sacrifices my wife and I had to make in order to raise them but we made many. There were times when I had to ask the Lord when He was going to step in for there was not enough money or time to do some of the things we had to do along the way.

We taught our children to pray each day and before they ate. No matter what we prayed for we wanted our children to know they needed to keep faith in God no matter what they prayed for. We taught them that God won't always give you what you ask for because not everything we ask for is what we need. God will sometimes not give us something to protect us from a certain thing or a certain person. Then there are other times God won't give us a certain thing for it was not the right time to get it or to be in a certain situation.

When our son went away to college, I told him there would be challenges but he should pray often and always keep in faith in God. He may have made decisions that I would have strongly disagreed with but I accepted it for I know he had to mature as a man and be able to make decisions on his own. I told him on many occasions that when situations seem to be bad, God is still with him and he should not give up on what God has him to do.

My wife and I knew when our son was very young that he had an interest in airplanes and space related matters. We saw on many occasions where it was hard for him to make friends when he was younger for other kids wanted to talk about small things, he talked about airplanes and technical matters that was way beyond what the kids could understand. So, it came to no surprise that our son wanted to go to college for Aerospace Engineering. Our son graduated high school with a 3.7 GPA so he was eligible to go to college in Georgia for free with Georgia's Hope Scholarship; however, to our surprise he was not accepted into Georgia Tech University. I had to explain to him that with any program that was only taking let's say 100 students into a specialized program there would be many well qualified students that would not be accepted.

Now I can show how good God is. As our son was waiting for word from Georgia Tech he was contacted by Embry-Riddle Aeronautical University, which invited him to apply. I don't know the time between his hearing from Georgia Tech and Embry-Riddle but Embry-Riddle accepted him into their program! The blessing in this was that Embry-Riddle had the number one Aerospace Engineering program in the country! At that time, Georgia Tech's program was number two. This meant that in the midst of not being accepted into a program, God blessed him to get into the best program available. The only difference it made to us as parents was that instead of him going to school in our home state for free, we would have a tuition to pay. God gave me the peace to know he was going to the place he needed to be.

My son offered to apply for lesser programs in Georgia so the tuition would be free but I had to explain to him there was no purpose to settling for a degree you had no interest in that he probably would not have used. It would be a waste of time to get a degree in something just so you can say you have a degree. The program at Embry-Riddle proved to be a tough one. At one point, our son wanted to change his degree to Air Traffic Control since it was less demanding. There's nothing wrong with Air Traffic Control; however, to get that degree to run from a more demanding one is what quitters do and I did not want him to be a quitter because circumstances were tough. He graduated from Embry-Riddle in December 2014. His whole family was proud of him!

After all this goodness, the devil wanted to throw doubt in his face. His GPA from college was not has high as it was from high school so circumstances and statistics started making him doubt if he would be able to get a good job in this field. The speaker at his graduation indicated most of them should be able to get a job within three months if they didn't already have offers. After six months of looking but not finding a career-related job, our son began to start stressing out about his potential. God later blessed him to find a minimum wage job but I told him to look at that as being a blessing until he was able to find the right job.

God later blessed our son with two more jobs in succession, each bringing an increase in pay but it still was not the kind of money someone with a degree like his should be making. I told our son on many occasions to take his eyes off his circumstances and keep praying to God for answers, even if it was not what he was expecting. I told our son to not allow others to distract him from what God has for him. In the summer, 2015, our son was contacted by an engineering company that worked with aerospace development and maintenance. He went through telephone interviews and was told they wanted him but the position was on a proposed contract with the government. There were no formal offers other than them expressing an interest in him.

As our son waited to hear from this company, he worried for he was quickly refused by many of the other companies to which he applied and now these people seem to be delaying their response to him. In the meantime, our son loved the job he got at an automotive dealership. Like his father, our son loved cars and motorcycles so this job was ideal for him while he awaited his career job. Constant prayer assured me that God would deliver our son from his dilemma at the right time. I talked to him and prayed with him over the phone. Our son still looked for jobs and found different positions at the company to which he applied. He applied for two of the available jobs. He was contacted for an initial telephone interview with the recruiter and got a second interview with two managers.

Based on what he told me was said in the in-person interview, I knew they wanted to hire my son. I prayed about the situation and God had me a peace with my son going to work for this company. As I prayed with him over this, I can tell my son was wondering whether he should take the job. He had too many distractions with other people trying to get him to do things their way. I told him to accept help from people but only have his faith in God. God can use people to help you but people can also let you down. He was later sent an offer letter that I advised my son to accept the job, but it was his decision. I'm proud to say although it took my son nine months from the time he graduated to get a career job, it was in God's timing that it occurred. I pray he keeps his faith in God and do great things with this company or for whomever he works for in the future.

When my son accepted the job, he was brought in making about $8,000 less than his piers started. I told him God would bless him to catch up on the pay while he was on the job. Things happened with him there where he gained a level of experience that someone new to the job would not have received for many years. He later received a Master's Degree from Embry-Riddle and equitable pay raises. His experience and education enabled him to later get hired at another company with a 27% pay raise!

Psalms 40:1-3 (NLT) says, [1] I waited patiently for the LORD to help me, and he turned to me and heard my cry. [2] He lifted me out of the pit of despair, out of the mud and the mire. He set my feet on solid ground and steadied me as I walked along. [3] He has given me a new song to sing, a hymn of praise to our God. Many will see what he has done and be amazed. They will put their trust in the LORD. This brings to mind that we sometimes do things or hesitate to do things based on hurt from our past or present. Many of use need to recover from bad situations and bad decisions in our lives. We need to get on our road to recovery.

The Road to Recovery

The road to recovery is full of bumps and scrapes, curves, and bends. You never know what to expect. The only sure thing you can count on is being able to turn to God with all your problems. God never promised us a life without problems when we give our lives to Him. God allows us to go through problems to build our character and sometimes to motivate us to make necessary changes in our lives. Psalm 25:9-13 (NLT) says, [9] He leads the humble in doing right, teaching them his way. [10] The LORD leads with unfailing love and faithfulness all who keep his covenant and obey his demands. [11] For the honor of your name, O LORD, forgive my many, many sins. [12] Who are those who fear the LORD? He will show them the path they should choose. [13] They will live in prosperity, and their children will inherit the land. Psalm 31:15 (NLT) says, [15] My future is in your hands. Rescue me from those who hunt me down relentlessly.

Many of us are constantly seeing doors being closed before us. However, we must realize that there could be many reasons doors are closed. Doors could have been closed to keep your past from catching up with you. We all have pasts that we don't need to revisit. Some doors are closed to keep your enemies from coming after you. In the past, God has closed doors because He didn't want His people to go back into Egypt.

Some of us are living in constant pain. Believe it or not, God wants to recycle your pain. God can use your pain to help others. All you have to do is share your story with others so they can see how you got through your pain. They can then use your example as inspiration that they can get through their problems.

Some of you may ask, why has God allowed my pain? I've already mentioned that God can use your pain to not only help you but to also help others. You should ask, how can I use my pain to help others? First you must realize that God uses pain to get your attention. You can then ask God what changes in your life God wanted you to make or what direction your should go.

We're supposed to be here to show the world God's light; it's not supposed to be the other way around. We sometimes act deliberately to not insult others that we begin to act more like them just so we can fit in. Jeremiah 15:18 - 19 (NLT) says, [18] Why then does my suffering continue? Why is my wound so incurable? Your help seems as uncertain as a seasonal brook, like a spring that has gone dry." [19]This is how the LORD responds: "If you return to me, I will restore you so you can continue to serve me. If you speak good words rather than worthless ones, you will be my spokesman." You must influence them; do not let them influence you!

You should never hesitate to tell others how you recovered from your problems or how you're in the process of recovering. Even if others don't want to hear your story or want you to share God's love, you should do it anyway for God offers comfort to all. The verses 2 Corinthians 1:3 - 5 (NLT) says, [3]All praise to God, the Father of our Lord Jesus Christ. God is our merciful Father and the source of all comfort. [4]He comforts us in all our troubles so that we can comfort others. When they are troubled, we will be able to give them the same comfort God has given us. [5]For the more we suffer for Christ, the more God will shower us with his comfort through Christ.

You should be proud of how you have faith that God will deliver you from your problems, even if you can't personally see your way out! Having faith in God is the best way to get through anything you're dealing with. You should never faint from telling your story. 1 Peter 3:15

(NLT) says, [15]Instead, you must worship Christ as Lord of your life. And if someone asks about your Christian hope, always be ready to explain it.

In late 2015, I was being seen by a new doctor at MacDill Air Force Base (AFB) clinic. She had put me through a series of tests checking on how my body was responding to blood pressure and cholesterol medicines. She told me everything looked fine but she was concerned about an elevated Prostate Specific Antigen (PSA) level. I had never heard of a PSA and she had to explain to me what it was. The best level would be a zero but mine was a 6.38. She had me go see a specialist off base.

At the specialist doctor's office, they checked my PSA and it was then a 6.18, which was a slight improvement but the doctor said he wanted to run more tests. He performed in simple exam and said he felt a small spot on my prostate that he wanted to do some biopsies on my prostate to determine if there was cancer. After the biopsies came back, he found cancer cells on 70% of the samples they took. The levels were low with the exception of one level that was considered "intermediate". The doctor gave me a few options from monitoring the levels to see if they would go up, radiation therapy which wasn't guaranteed, and finally surgery to remove my prostate. The last option (surgery) was the option my doctor thought was best for me.

After much prayer, talking it over with my family, and consulting with my primary doctor, I decided to take the surgical option. I knew this was a rather radical option for someone with the beginning stages of cancer but I felt it was the best option. I knew God would bring me through this time in my life. In February 2016 I had surgery for a total prostate removal. The surgery went well and my specialist doctor was surprised to see how quickly I was recovering in the hospital. I later had one setback that kept me in the hospital one more day than I expected. After that, God blessed me to recover quickly. My wife came to Florida from our home in Georgia to take care of me during and after my surgery. She remained at the hospital the whole time I was there.

I had to ensure some of the complications the doctors warned me about such as incontinence. The Lord blessed me to get over that in a short amount of time and I felt I did the right thing to extend the life God had blessed me with. One day after I came back from one of my follow-ups with the doctor my wife and I had an argument and it was not a good morning. Something told us to go to the food court on MacDill Air Force Base, FL even though neither of us really felt like eating. Now here comes another blessing. As we were entering the line at Taco Bell, one of the employees looked at my wife and starting screaming and yelling my wife's first name. It turned out to be an old friend of my wife that worked for my wife when my wife was an assistant manager many years ago at a local Taco Bell that was close to the base.

This run-in at Taco Bell occurred on the last week before I was due to take my wife back to Georgia. Before she came to Florida, she was a little depressed because she had looked for a job, got called back for a few interviews, but was not able to land a job. The employee told my wife there was a manager opening at this Taco Bell and she suggested my wife apply. My wife didn't apply until the next day. The day following her application she was called for an interview and got the job! God is so good! We traveled to Georgia to get some more of my wife's stuff and she moved to Florida to be with me and work her new job. My wife wasn't even looking for jobs in Florida at that time. God will open doors for you when you least expect. You just have to be willing to step through the door. After the recovery, God blessed me to become cancer free! It was confirmed again in April 2020 that I am still cancer free. No matter what happens in the future, my faith is in God!

Beware though for there will always be those who are willing to berate you and belittle your story. First, you need to know that in order to share a story, you must be humble. You must never appear to be bragging or putting others down because they don't have your blessings. Some people will even plot to destroy you or give you an undeserved bad reputation. Some will even try to hinder your progress at your job or business. Genesis 50:20 (NLT) shows us how all this matter: [20]You intended to harm me, but God intended it all for good. He brought me to this position so I could save the lives of many people.

Some of these folks are acting on what I've heard some preachers refer to as being "hindering spirits". Hindering spirits are designed to hinder God's plan for your life. People that were once helping can later become hindering spirits. At the beginning of time one of God's angels, Lucifer, fell from grace and started working against the kingdom of God.

Most of us have heard the great Bible stories of the life of Jesus and the many wonderful things he did for us. I think God's highest goal is for us to be like Jesus. Jesus' example should be inspiration for us the do more for others and use our God-given talents to show the light of Jesus inside us. We should look at ourselves and be thankful for what God has blessed us to become. We may not be all that we want to be but if we follow God, it will lead to a great future.

I say this knowing that no matter what, we must all face difficult times in our lives. God has placed others in our lives to help us in times of need. Some of them may be there to give good advice while others will help you pray your way through hard times. Ecclesiastes 4:12 (NLT) says, [12]A person standing alone can be attacked and defeated, but two can stand back-to-back and conquer. Three are even better, for a triple-braided cord is not easily broken. God has described our necessary bond with others as a three-stranded cord. This simply means when we bond with others in prayer or standing up to the devil, it makes us stronger than dealing with things alone. Sometimes dealing with things alone leads to discouragement, depression, and distraction. Watch out for your relationships and make sure they are lifting you up, not bringing you down.

Now back to the story with our son. Our son went to college in 2010. He had a small scholarship for $2500 each semester that helped in sending him to school. He didn't tell me he was having trouble keeping up in a few of his classes until it was too late. As a result of his lowered GPA, the school took away his scholarship and said he could not reapply until one year had passed. I prayed about this situation for that was money he earned and I needed to help towards his education. The Lord led me to call the school and explain his situation. They told me he usually would have to wait but if we submitted a written explanation of why his GPA was low and what he planned to do to fix it, they may reconsider. I had never done anything like this before but God told me some of the things he should include in his letter to the school. My son initially thought his effort would be hopeless. I'll have you know, there is always hope in God. Guess what - they gave him his scholarship back the following semester! Stay in God's Will and you will be blessed!

Riding Out/Living Through Your Current Season for a Breakthrough

There are just seasons in life we just have to stay faithful and live through them. Nehemiah 9:19-21 (NLT) tells us the story about the Hebrews' lives as they traveled to the promised land. [19]"But in your great mercy you did not abandon them to die in the wilderness. The pillar of cloud still led them forward by day, and the pillar of fire showed them the way through the night. [20]You sent your good Spirit to instruct them, and you did not stop giving them manna from heaven or water for their thirst. [21]For forty years you sustained them in the wilderness, and they lacked nothing. Their clothes did not wear out, and their feet did not swell!

There are different things we have to deal with in different environments as we live our lives. You're not the only person living in your environment. For example, the desert has its inhabitants, an environment that is usually hostile but the desert's inhabitants know how to live in it. It's more than the common analogy of dog eat dog. Oftentimes the solution to your problem is not a change in environment, but a change in you. Everything will change when you change.

Your attitude towards your life and the people you deal with makes a big difference in your life. You've heard the expression before that your attitude determines your altitude. You have to have a positive outlook and some determination to get to where God wants you to be. Your destiny is not just a process, it's a series of events and seasonal growth that develops you as a person.

You must be able to tell yourself you're a lot more than your situation or circumstances in your life dictate. You must act on what you acknowledge. Acknowledge that you're special in God's eyes and you can be faithful and go in the direction that God sends you. There is a turning point coming in your life and you can't get to it by sitting still and waiting for something to happen. Pray to God as to what He wants you to do. Also look deep in your heart and see what God has placed there. When you see what you want to be, go for it! You can only succeed if you have faith. Your faith knows something that's beyond what you can see. Do something out of faith!

Sometimes even doing things out of faith can be frustrating. All of your efforts are not in vain even though some of them will fail. Once I realized that we would keep our family home in Georgia, something inside me wanted to purchase a smaller home to keep from having to pay rent the entire time I would be in Florida. There was the older house that was built around 1954 that I used to see as I ran along Westshore Boulevard in Tampa, FL. I liked the house for it had a huge shed out back big enough to fit my car and motorcycles. The house had been on the market for a while so I eventually got a realtor and took a look at the house.

I knew at that time that my credit needed some repair but thought I would apply anyway. My application was denied for my credit score was too low at that time. I really felt disappointed whenever I ran past the house and eventually it was sold. One day as I was running past the house again instead of disappointment, I got a good feeling. The Lord told me not to feel bad for he had something better for me. I had no idea as to what the Lord was talking about. I knew I had become comfortable living in South Tampa and within 3.9 miles from my job. God had blessed me with a nice apartment in a complex that looked like a resort.

A few times over I ran across houses that I really liked but I didn't get a feeling for them. There was another house I used to see that was on a very large lot and it had a pool in the back with a lanai. There was something special about that house it was not for sale but you could tell no one lived there but the grass was always cut. I later saw a sign indicated the property was being managed by a company. During the time I had my surgery the house was placed on the market for sale. Based on the photos I realized that this was a very nice house. My wife called the number on the sign but the realtor was not very friendly and demanded we get pre-approved before he would show us the house. I told him if he had conditions for us seeing the house then I'm not going to take the time to apply for anything when I was only interested in that house and had not decided to buy, especially since we had never seen the inside of the house.

Along the way I saw some townhouses being built on my route from work. I really liked the way they were being built for they had cement block construction all the way to the second floor. I thought that was great for most of the block construction houses being built nearby only had cement blocks on the first floor and it was wood-framed on the second floor. I was also impressed by the fact there were concrete block between each unit. As I stopped to take a look there was a guy standing near the end of the dirt driveway and he came up to my car. He apologized for he thought I was someone else. I asked him about the buildings and later found out he was the builder. I later felt it was not coincidence that I met the guy building the project. This was in November of 2015. I later talked to the guy again in December 2015.

The project was supposed to be finished in January 2016 but he was delayed due to different issues. In the meantime, I was praying the Lord help me get my credit score back up. One minute it was up and then something else happened with creditors beyond my control that brought it back down. I applied for a credit card with a back with whom I had an account that would have boost my credit score. I was denied for the card.

When the Lord placed it on my mind to apply for buying one of the townhouses, I couldn't help but to think on the fact I was denied a house loan the previous year and recently denied the credit card. I was being considered for a promotion that would have sent me to Virginia but things were laying on my heart that showed me the move would have messed my family situation up for I would have been further away from home and my cost of living would have gone up. After much prayer, I called a friend of mine and asked not to be considered for the promotion. After realizing I'd done what the Lord led me to do, I prayed to him that now that I'm in compliance I needed him to show himself in my situation.

Shortly after that and to my surprise my wife told me to go ahead and apply for a loan for the new townhouse. I thought to myself initially this would be impossible for I would then owe more on this townhouse than I did on the mortgage for our family home in Georgia. God had a friend provide insight as to where I should apply for a home loan for the new townhouse in Tampa. When I applied for the townhouse loan, I clearly told them I had no intention of selling our house in Georgia. God's Grace and Mercy came through for us one more time! We were approved for the loan! God blessed me to be approved at a time when most folks would think they wouldn't qualify. There was difficulty in moving forward on the townhouse purchase but God guided us through it. This place was even closer to my job than my apartment. There were a few stumbles with the builder for our unit was the first one to be contracted in that set of homes. God is the master of possibilities when things seem impossible!

Then there was the situation we went through trying to close on the new home. This is a testimony of how God knows what's better for us even though we don't understand why we are experiencing different difficult moments and situations. We were initially scheduled to close on our new home on June 23, 2016. At that time my closing cost was about $1600 since I was using a VA loan. We were later informed that due to some difficulty in their compiling documentation and lack of responses from other parties, our closing date would be moved to about June 28, 2016. If we closed on that date, our closing cost would then be only $745. I was quite irritated for I also had to deal with trying to get out of my apartment by the end of June to avoid paying July 2016 rent.

I prayed to God about what I should do for now I would not have any help in my move if I had to move during the week. God showed me we should move out on the weekend of 24 June 2016 and stay in a hotel until we got to close. God showed me the way of renting a truck to load and store our furniture until we got to close. No other storage solution seemed to fit our situation. As the week of 27 June 2016 began, we were told that our close date had been moved to June 30, 2016. I thought this to be a problem for I had not rented the truck that long and I had to extend our stay at the hotel. I called the rental truck company on the night of 29 June 2016 to extend the truck until 1 July 2016. The answering service said they would pass along my request. On 30 June 2016, I got a call from the truck rental company that I could not extend the truck another day. They had rented it out to another party that was due to pick it up around 11:30am. Based on their policy, I already owed a $50 late return fee since I had gone past 8:00am. It was about 9:30am at the time I got the call. Frantic, I left work to go get the truck where I had parked it. I called my builder to see if he knew of any day laborers, I could hire to offload the truck. As God would work it, my builder and one of the guys that worked for me volunteered to help me offload into the garage of the townhome even though we had not closed yet. I got the truck unloaded and turned in without a penalty. That, to me, was a blessing! What I didn't know was that God was working in the background to bless us.

I then got a call from the bank letting me know that our closing would now be on 1 July 2016. I was quite mad by this time and told the bank representative that they were about to make us homeless for I had already moved out of the apartment. He told me that unfortunately that was our only choice. I told the representative that the problem was with my closing at the beginning of the month. That would mean I would have to pay more in closing cost (of which I didn't have). He told me that since I was originally set to have to pay my first mortgage note on the new townhouse in August 2016, he could make it where I would not have to pay all the first month's expense. This is where God showed his favor! As a result of the all the credits I received and due to the VA loan, instead of me having to pay closing cost at closing, the bank owed us money! At closing, they wrote us a check! The servicing title company representative and my realtor said this was highly unusual that I would receive money at closing instead of having to pay.

You see, I could only see what I was dealing with and did not understand what God was doing. You should keep the faith and let God do what only God can do. Yes, sometimes you have to step back and let go and stop trying to control everything!

One of the last stories I'd like to discuss here happened from November to December 2018. I had a wonderful 2007 Lexus GS 450h but I knew it was no longer serving the purposes I needed in a road car. I already had a good commuter car, a motorcycle, and a scooter for the short distance driving. God started showing me a vehicle that could fit my needs and more. I had previously been looking for a pickup truck but I knew as soon as I purchased one, I would have to cover the bed to fit my needs. The pickup truck that I found was nice but it was too slow for my taste and I thought I could overcome that due to the good gas mileage of this particular truck.

The only problem with the truck other than it being too slow was that it was a diesel and for the kind of driving I would do; the diesel engine would cause me problems for I would do a lot of idling and I've read reports that show this vehicle had a lot of problems if idled too long. But I still wanted the truck due to its looks and high gas mileage. I began to see where other conditions with the truck would cause me to be unhappy with it later.

During the same time, I experienced a situation with my motorcycle where I almost dropped it because my legs were too short to move it backwards with comfort and my foot slipped on some small rocks the last time I drove it to work. Both my car and motorcycle were paid for so that kept me from making a move for quite some time. I went by a local motorcycle dealership I frequent occasionally just to look and sometimes bought accessories I wanted. They had some 2018 Goldwings on clearance and were selling their top of line model for $4500 off. I knew this was a good deal but I had to do some research. I checked around and up in Atlanta and found out the best I could do at those places was $2850 off.

I knew from past experience that I would not qualify if I applied for a motorcycle loan through the dealership. I applied for a loan through an online company my son recommended and they denied the loan. I prayed about this situation and God told me He would bless me. I didn't know how He would do it so I left it alone for a bit. I felt God was leading me to apply at one of the credit unions I was a member of. This particular credit union had just given me a loan to replace my daughter's car that someone had crashed into and the insurance money alone was not enough to get a reliable car (another blessing we can discuss at another time). So, I was hesitant to go back to them. I applied for the loan and as I was sitting in front of the loan officer, the devil had me thinking negatively and I said to myself that it was taking too long and it meant the loan would not be approved. I had to stop and say Lord forgive me for doubting You. The negativity left and shortly thereafter, the loan officer advised me the loan had been approved. I then had a preapproved loan to go get the motorcycle but I was still dealing with the issue of whether I should by a crossover vehicle I had been wanting for some time.

My story is not to encourage anyone to go and get into debt. I just know the Lord has a tendency to show through me His ability to provide no matter what my credit score or financial situation is. I also knew that should the Lord bless me with either vehicle, He would bless me with a means to pay for it. Quite frankly, I thought it would be like what had happened to me in the past where I never had to make payments on a certain loan.

I went to Georgia for my granddaughter's second birthday. I had been looking for a Ford Flex with the twin turbo engine, which were hard to find. I found one at a dealership in Tampa but it was being driven by the dealership's owner's wife and they could never find the keys when I went to drive it before making a decision. Also, it was black and I didn't want a black vehicle, especially in Florida. This happened again on my second time going to this dealership. They tried to sell me one of the other Ford Flexes but they didn't have the equipment I wanted on it. I think their not being able to find the keys was a blessing for me for I didn't want to buy something just because it was the only one available.

While I was visiting my home in Georgia and after some research there, I found a dealership outside of Atlanta had one that was in transit. It was a beautiful red that was almost the color of the motorcycle I wanted. Since I didn't live there, I wasn't going to call to see when it was scheduled to arrive. Something told me to call them anyway. The salesman told me the vehicle was still in transit but he would check to see when it would arrive. He then told me to hold on a minute. When he came back to the phone, he said he knew he had saw something that morning when the delivery truck arrived. He thought it was funny that the vehicle I inquired about had arrived the same morning I called. I stopped by this dealership on my way back to Tampa and loved the vehicle. My grandson, who was traveling with me, also loved the vehicle. The dealership was willing to give me more on my trade than anyone else had. I told them that I had to pray about it for I knew financing was going to be an issue and I wasn't an impulsive buyer.

I prayed about this situation most of the way back to Tampa. God was assuring me it was all OK and He was willing to bless me. I went ahead and applied for an auto loan with the dealership that Sunday night. I knew it was a longshot but by faith, I did it anyway. I questioned why I would consider this move since my car, a 2007 Lexus GS 450h was paid for. I knew though that the Lexus was no longer filling my needs for I didn't have room for the stuff I liked to travel with and to add passengers and their luggage was a pain.

I also knew when God put me up to something there was a reason for it. The last time I hesitated on doing something God was leading me to do, it cost me money I could not recover later. Two days later I contacted the dealership to see what was the status and they said they were still working on finding someone that would finance the vehicle for me. In the meantime, rejection letters started arriving at the house in Georgia. When I called them three days after I applied, I told them that I only applied for the loan because I felt God had led me to do so but if they thought they would place me with a high-risk finance company with a high interest rate, they could stop for I was not willing to do that. I got a call later that day from the dealership's finance director who explained to me that they were not trying to put me in a high-interest car payment. He said he heard I was a man of faith and so was he, and he was hoping my prayers were answered even though all recent banks had turned me down. We ended that call with my feeling good about who I was dealing with.

I got a call from the dealership's finance director on day 4 after I applied and said that to his delight, a bank had approved financing for me to purchase the vehicle. I was elated but still concerned about going into debt but God assured me not to worry. I told him thanks for I had to pray about it and I would let them know. That night I prayed for God to guide me for now I didn't know which vehicle to purchase, the motorcycle or the Ford Flex. I got an answer – you can have them both! I asked God how in the world can I do that and He assured me again not to worry. I ended up purchasing both vehicles at reduced prices! God is so good!

My wife was not happy with my decisions and wondered how I would pay for it. I told her hopefully it would be like what God had done in the past where I would be blessed with the money before the notes were due. If not, God would make a way. Well, the time for payments came and I managed to pay them; however, I wondered if this was going to be a regular thing. I knew what God had told me but as I've always said, God's timing is not our timing.

I've had to make some sacrifices to make the payments for now but God has made a way. I'm still looking for the Lord's blessing me to pay the two vehicle loans and some student loans off.

Breakthrough!

I had been getting ready for my second retirement but didn't know what I'd do next. Nor did I know from where the money would come for the debts such as student loans. I didn't tell many people beyond my wife about problems in finances I had been experiencing. I told the Lord my needs and knew he would come through.

The last week of November 2019 something told me to apply at St. Leo University for a teaching position. I was able to call the accreditation department at the school and found out they did not have any online positions available but did have a position on a ground course in Tampa. I then started the process of applying and asked three friends of mine for letters of recommendation. One friend provided one the same day I asked and another a couple of days later. The final one came in while I was on Thanksgiving leave with my family. I don't know what God led me to do this but I'm sure there was purpose behind it. I was blessed to have been placed on the list of adjunct professors. God amazes me like that!

A friend of mine told me they sent me a letter to my address in Tampa, FL. When I got home from my trip to

Georgia, I opened my mail and found out my friend had sent me a check for $400. What?! I got on the phone and thanked my friend to doing that and said I didn't know what led my friend to send me the money but I thanked God for that inspiration. This money meant more than the additional money for me to use, it also meant God was showing me He had the resources to bless me no matter what I was able to see. I paid my tithes on this money and took care of other things with the rest.

I held off publishing this book since I was waiting for a blessing from God where I would pay off loans for both my new car and my new motorcycle. That hadn't happened yet but I still know God will deliver. I continued to pray that God would work the loan issues out for me. In the meantime, there were new rule issued on my retirement plan that would allow us to take money out of the retirement fund. I had just made it in to qualifying for this process. I talked to my wife about it and we both agreed to take advantage of the opportunity. The blessing was we were able to withdraw from the account and we used the money to pay off the mortgage on our Georgia house! God is so good! Even though it took quite a bit out of our account, we still had enough to still receive a monthly income after I retire.

You wouldn't believe the pushback we got from the mortgage company when I made the payment. To make a long story short, we went from being a couple of months behind on our payments to paying the house off in a little over fourteen years! I've made a point some time ago that we believers need to stop tying God's hands by telling Him how to bless us. There is nothing wrong with telling God your needs or your wants. Just understand that God can and will bless you in more than the ways and means you are familiar with. I had no idea I would get a chance to just pay off our mortgage without having won the lottery or something like that. I will continue to walk through the fire of life and be forged in that fire so long as I'm following the Lord in all I do. Be willing to walk through the fires of life and allow God to forge you to become all He wants you to be. I highly encourage you to follow Godly principles in all aspects of your life and you too will be blessed.